Umbra:philia

for the shadow lovers.

ear Andy,

eab bo share space wllbh you

his meek ab Arvon.

nrks for bhe workshops,

1ocnce, support + hspration.

love Sonie X

Umbra:philia

Sonia Burns

BEARDED BADGER
PUBLISHING CO.

Contents

Solar Eclipse, Brunei, 1986

I am moonchild; translucent.
Riding my red BMX -
E.T, not Elliott.

Homeless hermit in a new world,
a prehistoric landscape of mangroves
and monitor lizards.

Gentle constellations of freckles
on shoulders, soon pink and blistered.

School starts at seven -
by midday we hide, equator-hot
and sunscreen-sticky, shadow lovers
retreating to coolness inside.

Here, night falls like a guillotine.
We see shooting stars, Halley's comet -
tail untangled from Hydra

and once the dark dares its way into daylight,
the moon a talisman; eclipsing everything -
solid as a crab's shell.

Breech*

Rupturing your way into the world, arse over tit.
Indulging in risky behaviour from the start.
Not quite ready to commit.

You scream into the pillow of your mother's body.
She is a breakwater, sheltering your soft skull
from the horrors of the everyday.

Your birth is a rift in the universe;
a fissure in the rock of your parents' reality.
You whisper that you don't want to leave, not yet

because you are *the one who knows*
and you are not ready for this dawn.

In Bolivia, Yatiri, meaning 'the one who knows' are healers usually elected to the position by supernatural events, one of which is being born breech.

Hand Me Down

I can see you now, your green armchair in the corner,

ashtray on the arm.

Perpetual cigarette in hand, haze of smoke and face powder

blurring your outline.

Glasses on a chain around your neck.

Smartly dressed, faultlessly coiffed and set.

After you died the room smelled like you for years, through
countless coats of paint.

You were a great one for games.

Weekly bingo, never without a puzzle book; a Sudoku pioneer.

Good with words, always ready with a funny turn of phrase,

telling me; *little pickers wear big knickers*

as you pass me the wooden spoon to scrape the bowl clean.

We'd collect blackcurrants together, from the bushes at the bottom of the garden.

Your jam is still legendary, 13 years on, although someone else picks those berries now.

Mealtimes you'd spend on your feet, cheerfully looking after us all but late at night you'd sit smoking in the kitchen, alone in the dark.

Tracing lines on palms which spelled out grandmother

and matriarch.

Holding that picture of Uncle Frank, so handsome,

in black and white.

Comfort Zone

I am a black hole in your galaxy,
absorbing your universe.
A star in your
sea-blue
sky.

My frilled and suckered
thoughts swim, alive
with sensation.

573 + 66 x coral + pink
purple, green and shimmer;
sudden movement?
Freeze.

Growing to fill the void
and growing and growing.
When I fit too snugly
I know it is time
to find
a new
space.

Network 23

We move as one, a prime number, two and three entwined
together, flaunting Satan's symbol, devil dancing at Teknivals,
cloven hooves pounding a rhythm - vibrating from Castlemorton
to Europe and beyond.

We follow each other to free parties in fields, on beaches in Wales,
in woods and at abandoned power stations, as our young years
pass by, time moving as quickly as the blood beating through
our slim bodies.

We learn community, communication, anarchy and wild
experimentation. Our minds take flight, find freedom soaring
over abandoned air strips, creating autonomous states

we are a little duck being eaten by a snake.
Signed up for life, dissent our happy place, swallow our stash
in a Glasgow warehouse. Reclaim the Streets with cans of blood-
red paint to helicopter beats; *Forward the Revolution.*

We get messy and see worse, our marbles scattered on wooden
floors. Return to comfortable homes with imaginations aflame,
in awe of those who live it, who teach us what alternative means.

Photo Album

Here we are, looking like Sid and Nancy,
life speeding past unnoticed,
gazing into each other's navels.

Here we are in the pub, playing
Fake Plastic Trees on the jukebox,
again, drinking Black Russians,
underage in dark corners.

Here we are, hanging out
in your friend's car in the college car park,
smoking and watching Neighbours
on his portable TV. He has a pager too.
I sit in the back.

Here you are, with your politician smile,
casually cruel, holding yourself just out of reach,
realising your full potential.
Here I am, recognising for the first time,
the chasm between men and women.

Here we are, legs dangling
over the side of an empty swimming pool,
smoking Royals down to the butt,
talking all night, yellow-fingered
and dry mouthed.

Here you are, hood up, gaze lowered,
blowing smoke towards me like an ambush.
Here I am, drinking in graveyards
and crying, pissing behind
walls.

Here we are, looking like Bonnie and Clyde,
mouths pursed in disapproval, feeling black and white
on a Tuesday.

Here we are, obliterating ourselves
before we're even fully formed, like burning photographs
of children.

Here you are, hiding under the covers
and saying *I just want to be normal.*

Here we are, seeing things that aren't there.

Here I am.
Missing you with all the parts of me that are forever 18.
Here I still am.

Winter

The river rises
Saturates cold ground
Tea brews bitter

Weak as water
Deluge of disease
Swamps your cells

Benches are submerged
Fish in puddles
Drown and float

Flooding

Cancer drugs course
Through your body
Nails turn black

Flow of poison
Rush of sickness
Kill to cure

Needles in veins
Plump with toxins
Flush it out

Nowhere to go
Too much pressure
Bursts your banks

Inconceivable

Because you are a dead end.
A cul-de-sac, where there is no one
home, an abandoned bicycle
on a lawn, wheels spinning
slowly in afternoon sunlight.
Because you are vacant;
a cold water flat with no tenant,
a *To Let* sign behind your eyes,
waiting for a visitor
you don't remember inviting.
Because you are unbroken code,
an enigma which will remain
unsolved, impenetrable jargon,
hieroglyphics; womanhood
written in invisible ink.

Because you are barren
and bewildering; the frozen maze
at the end of *The Shining*,
a caretaker who does not care,
a lonely song with a sad ending.
Because you are as shallow
as a puddle on a farmyard track,
a pond where the frogspawn
will never hatch, no Moses basket
hidden in your rushes;
Ophelia drowning
amongst your water lilies.
Because you are lost blueprint,
unflicked switch; a biological
clock which does not tick.
A hand grenade with the pin intact
slowly corroding as the years pass.

Pomegranates

That holiday
straight off the plane
we witness a motorbike crash in Antalya.

The next day we wake in a white-walled room
to Brexit, rushing to a cashpoint
before the pound can sink any further.

At the coast, fire surges from a spark
carelessly dropped in dry brush.
Smoke noose tightens and chokes,
helicopters dip the Mediterranean.

Snorkelling all day to forget the world
we swim with turtles, eat fish on the boat,
returning to reports of a bomb
in Istanbul airport.

We marvel at pomegranates
dripping from the trees, split one open,
drink its juice on the beach
and despite everything, this feels like paradise.

Ode to England

You are darkly compelling, repellent;
a seagull pecking through five pm vomit.

You are cigarette butts and shops shut up,
stolen bikes and optimistic scooters
broken and abandoned on your street corners.

You are an empty plastic swing, in a garden
sloping steeply down to another busy road.

You are daylight drug deals
round the back of takeaways,
motorways and fly-tipped lay-bys,
scaffolding and boarded up buildings,
codeine dependency and long-term sickness,
fat men in football shirts with unfinished business;
your stale air crackles with violence.

Adorned with betting shops and B&M bargains
you guard your monuments to abhorrence.

You are stasis; the same after forty years,
you are filthy carpets and piss-stained floors.
You are constant struggle with little reward;

a woman pushing a buggy up a hill
day after day
again and again.

Threefold

I exist in trifold, triplicate universes;

pale fingers touching through glass.
                 Sibling stars orbit one another -
blood *troika*, bonded together.

                Pale fingers touching through glass,
mental connections travel light years;
              same imaginations - brains won't switch off.

Sibling stars orbit one another -
              echoing planets with similar landscapes.
We share red hair, freckles, light eyes.

              Blood *troika*, bonded together,
we are each other's beginning and end;
             strength in numbers; familiar dimensions.

Audio Signal Processing

Avoid site kids with eyes like bad trips. Circumvent
caravans crowded with self-proclaimed shamans
weaving robot folklore and witch-stitched LSD.
Watch weekend people arrive, lipstick-fresh in shiny cars,
destined for loss. Listen to a dial tone from nowhere;
sound of the void, of mistakes made.
Shake skeleton maracas over chords of hope,
sinister swell builds until it swallows you whole.
Brush off sonic insects; aphids in the garden of acid.
Explore caverns of sound, dripping disembodied voices.
Tell machine fairy tales, brain scoured empty and clean;
the comfort of rhythm like finding lost selves in a dream.
Dig beats warped by green hills; vibrations boom
muffled from inside soft mounds of dark earth;
syncopated snores of sleeping giants.
Drum up dust with throbbing, breakbeat energy,
sound semaphoring patterns of grief and joy;
no sense of space like a dance floor beneath metal skies.

Leopard Prints

after Ciarán Hodgers / for Becky

Leopard-light, you leave no prints,
hula-hooping in sequins,
earrings graze your collarbone.
Breathing fire through paraffin prisms.

Red wine-stained lips and lives,
Irish coffee at strange times,
impossible to stay asleep
hungover, heart pounding.

Gardening, green-fingered
dirty nails and sunburnt skin.
Pink-cheeked babies bring sorrow;
mothering with nowhere to go.

Tea and roll-ups in beige caffs
wine on tick from corner shops.
Blurred days, inappropriate men,
feather boas, leopard print.

Purple-bruised and prowling,
mountain bike marauding.
Twitching, you know every bird.
Stuff borrowed and not returned.

Peaches, oranges, apricots.
An agony of choice.
Let down yellow-gold hair,
trapped in your tower of bones.

Blue veins map the miles you walk
carrying rocks and scales.
Disobey nature, switch off hunger;
loneliness grows on your skin like fur.

Tidings

after One for Sorrow - the magpie nursery rhyme

I.

Salute me.
Mutter spells
born on dead tongues.

I am your talisman.

II.

I provide the ultimate
contrast; chiaroscuro.

You vibrate to my frequency.
Connection soars like sound.

III.

My treasures are older
than diamonds or pearls.

I feather my nest with the boa
you left on the back
of that deckchair on the lawn.

I make my home
in your glass slipper.

IV.

Blue is a state of mind.
Stoicism is my shell.
I cannot peck
my way free
of masculinity.

V.

The setting sun
on the lake, evensong,
a tiny bell signalling
the end of everything.

A feeling that it wasn't so bad
after all, because we had
each other and we laughed
a lot, didn't we?

VI.

Keep it buried, or melt it down?

Boxes of keepsakes you hoard
but never look at.
Ticket-stub crumbs collected.
Ballast, because without stuff
you are all too ready
to return to the void.

Your collections keep you safe
and make you solid.

VII.

The constant chittering
of life, like the robotic trill
of a lonely car alarm.

I sing a song from the future,
of rivers of plastic and fields of death.

The smell of forgotten tubers
rotting in the thaw
reveals itself to the air
like a long-held secret.

The truth is in the telling.

A Touch of the Old Magic

It is the same but smaller -
the inflatable giraffe bouncy castle droops a little now
as I droop, in the surprising heat,
queueing for a cone outside Morelli's
behind children hyped up on sugar-anticipation.

The breeze is empty, caressing, muting the hubbub inside,
where it is the 1950s, all pink and pearl and gleaming sundae
glasses, marbled Formica and soft banquettes.
Silver ashtrays adorn pavement tables and red neon exclaims
at the sunshine, through a haze of petrol fumes and piss.

In the distance, a tiny person paddles out to sea on a board,
against waves which glitter like a promise.

I get my cone and walk the promenade,
past 20p slots and memorial benches,
a round-faced boy smirks at his friend
as they sit on *in memory of Arthur Smith.*

Pistachio ice cream drips down my wrist.

I scan teenage names chalked on candy floss beach huts,
see 14-year-old me in a *Pixies* t-shirt -
whose name would I have scrawled, nearly 30 years ago?

A young couple drink pints of cold beer
and eat *frito misto* on the harbour wall,
an older couple on another bench eat cold chips in silence
and maybe they've done this every Saturday for a decade.

Families wrestle-dress reticent children
and I think about how my brothers hold their babies.

Kids call and seagulls screech and people play frisbee,
a man shouts *Let's see if he's still got it, a touch of the old magic!*
I breathe in seaweed and sun-baked rocks and watch the waves.
They just keep coming and coming and coming.

ACKNOWLEDGEMENTS

Thanks to:

My family and friends for inspiring, supporting and encouraging me always.

Arts Council England for awarding me the funding to support this project.

Leanne Moden and all the Paper Crane Poets.

The Wise Talk Collective – Camille McCawley, Helen Rice and Chris Single-ton, and the poets teaching the Wise Talk development programme – Jamie Thrasivoulou, Matt Abbott, Genevieve Carver.

Apples and Snakes.

Colin Bancroft,192 Magazine and the Poets Directory (Inconceivable was published in 192 as Time Bomb).

Open Collab (Charlie & Jake) for improvising a seaside soundscape for A Touch of the Old Magic.

Gill Lambert and Mark Connors for their Sunday Wordship workshops (where both Solar Eclipse and Breech started life).

All the Derby poets, Sophie Sparham, Charlotte Lunn, Tanvir Akram, True Colours, too many to mention, consider yourself mentioned. All the East Midlands poets, the UK poets, the global poets.

TRA[verse]

For more information about the range of poetry on the TRA[verse] imprint, please visit:

www.beardedbadgerpublishing.com

or follow us on social media:

Facebook - **Bearded Badger Publishing**

Twitter - **@beardedbadgerpc**

Instagram - **@bearded_badger_publishing**